A Lion Book
an imprint of
Lion Hudson plc
Mayfield House, 256 Banbury Road,
Oxford OX2 7DH, England
www.lionhudson.com
ISBN 13: 978 0 7459 5204 8
ISBN 10: 0 7459 5204 6

First edition 2006
10 9 8 7 6 5 4 3 2 1

Typeset in 11.5/14 Calligraph421
Printed and bound in Malaysia

Picture Acknowledgments

All pictures, unless noted below, by Digital Vision.
Alamy: pp. 26–27 (Steve Bloom), p. 35 (David Hoffman),
pp. 40–41 (Tim Street-Porter).

Jonathan Roberts: p. 42.

Text Acknowledgments

p. 11 *To be a Pilgrim*, Basil Hume OSB (Slough, St Paul
Publications, 1984)

p. 15 *Bread for the Journey*, Henri J M Nouwen (Darton, Longman
and Todd, 1996)

p. 23 *The Problem of Pain*, C S Lewis (London, HarperCollins, 1940)

pp. 32, 44 *Celtic Daily Prayer*, The Northumbria Community
(London, HarperCollins, 2000)

pp. 8, 11, 16, 17, 22, 23, 28, 32, 33, 36, 37, 38 , 43, 46 Scripture
quotations taken from the Holy Bible, New International Version,
copyright © 1973, 1978, 1984 International Bible Society. Used by
permission of Zondervan and Hodder & Stoughton Limited. All
rights reserved. The 'NIV' and 'New International Version'
trademarks are registered in the United States Patent and
Trademark Office by International Bible Society. Use of either
trademark requires the permission of International Bible Society.
UK trademark number 1448790.

pp. 12, 18 Scripture quotations are from the Contemporary English
Version published by The Bible Societies/HarperCollins Publishers,
copyright © 1991, 1992, 1995 American Bible Society.

pp. 13, 14 Scripture quotations taken from the The Message.
Copyright © 1993, 1994, 1995, 1996, 2000, 2001, 2002. Used by
permission of NavPress Publishing Group.

pp. 14, 20, 41, 42, 46 Scripture quotations are taken from the Holy
Bible, New Living Translation, copyright © 1996. Used by
permission of Tyndale House Publishers, Inc., Wheaton, Illinois
60189. All rights reserved.

p. 20 Psalm 23:4 taken from the English translation of the Jewish
Bible, the Tanach. Copyright © 1917 Jewish Publication Society.

p. 21 Extract from the Authorized Version of the Bible (The King
James Bible), the rights in which are vested in the Crown, are
reproduced by permission of the Crown's Patentee, Cambridge
University Press.

THE PILGRIM HEART

Written and compiled
by Liz Babbs

LION

Dedicated to
my mother Ann

CONTENTS

One does
not discover
new lands
without
consenting
to lose
sight of
the shore.

Andre Gide

INTRODUCTION

The road of life takes many twists and turns. There are mountain-tops of joy and celebration, but there are also valleys of pain and difficulty.

Maybe you're enjoying a mountain-top experience at the moment, or perhaps you're in a valley. It's often in the valleys that we learn most about ourselves and about God.

The Pilgrim Heart grew out of my own particular valley – the valley of burnout. But this valley proved to be a real investment for me because it taught me how to live my life at a different pace. I no longer bomb down the motorway of life driven by ambition, desperate to get to my destination as soon as possible. Instead, I build in time to venture along different pathways, enjoying the view.

My hope is that as you read this book you too might be encouraged to travel at a slower speed, setting time aside to explore more creative and restorative routes. And maybe you'll uncover new pathways rather than simply furrowing the same old ones. God created this world for our enjoyment, so don't wait for ill health to give you a reality check. Take stock now, and you too will discover the views across the hills are spectacular!

Blessed are those whose strength is in you,
who have set their hearts on pilgrimage.

Psalm 84:5

Every journey begins with a first step.

Margaret Silf

THE JOURNEY We may ask ourselves, 'Why am I here? Where am I going? What is my destination?' These are essentially spiritual questions to which we are all seeking answers.

When I was in my mid-twenties I seemed to have everything – a good job, a new car and my first house – and yet part of me remained unsatisfied. I found myself thinking that there had to be more to life than material possessions; there was something I was missing. I didn't realize it then, but what

I was searching for was a spiritual dimension to my life.
But it was only when tragedy struck my family that my
real search for God began.

Show me your ways, O Lord,
teach me your paths… for you are God my Saviour,
and my hope is in you all day long.

Psalm 25:4–5

The worst poverty today is the poverty of not having
spiritual values in life. It is more crippling than material
poverty.

Basil Hume

Whether you turn to the right or to the left,
your ears will hear a voice behind you, saying,
'This is the way; walk in it.'

Isaiah 30:21

We are so very small; we are at the foothills in our
understanding of God and His world. But it is good that we
should be at the foothills; that keeps us humble. Eventually
we shall get to the top of the mountain. We shall then see the
full vision.

Basil Hume

Only God is,
Only God knows,
Only God can do anything.

Carlo Carretto

Let nothing disturb you,
Nothing dismay you;
All things are passing;
God never changes;
Patient endurance
Attains all things;
Whoever possesses God
Lacks nothing:
God alone suffices.

Teresa of Avila

Even before I was born, you had written in your book
everything I would do.

Psalm 139:16

Be thou a bright flame before me,
Be thou a guiding star above me,
Be thou a smooth path below me,
Be thou a kindly shepherd behind me,
Today – tonight – and for ever.

St Columba

TRAVELLING LIGHT

Life is a journey, with a beginning, a middle and an end. But somewhere in the middle we tend to grow weary and lose sight of our destination.

The words 'destiny' and 'destination' are linked – those who know where they're heading are more likely to reach their goal. Many people today feel imprisoned by their circumstances and responsibilities and long to have

time out from the rat race of life. Maybe you'd like to have a desert island experience where you can escape for twenty-four hours from all your commitments. Well, even King David felt that need. Thousands of years ago he said, *'Get me out of here on dove's wings; I want a walk in the country, I want a cabin in the woods. I'm desperate for a change from rage and stormy weather'* (Psalm 55:6–8). God cares about our health and wants us to enjoy life. He says, *'Keep company with me and you'll learn how to live freely and lightly'* (Matthew 11:30).

WHO AM I?...

Am I just a cog
grinding against a wheel
squeezed into the machinery of life
where work dominates
and my spirit is quenched?

EROSION OF
SELF

As the waves crash
against the rocks
so negative thoughts
pound against the shoreline
of our personality
eroding our sense
of worth.

Don't get worked up about what may or may not
happen tomorrow,
God will help you deal with whatever hard things come up.

Matthew 6:34

What I'm trying to do here is to get you to relax, to not be so
preoccupied with getting, so you can respond to God's giving.

Matthew 6:31

If you want to know what God wants you to do – ask him,
and he will gladly tell you.

James 1:5

The Lord will guide you continually, watering your life when
you are dry and keeping you healthy, too.

Isaiah 58:11

I gird myself today with
The Power of God;
God's strength to comfort me;
God's wisdom to guide me;
God's ear to hear me;
God's word to speak to me;
God's hand to lead me;
God's shield to protect me.

St Patrick

'There is a great difference between
successfulness and fruitfulness…
Success brings many rewards and
often fame. Fruits, however, come from
weakness and vulnerability. And fruits
are conceived in vulnerability.'

Henri Nouwen

Sacred Space

When we make space for God we are satisfying a deep spiritual need to connect with the source of all life – our Creator Father.

That deep communion with God will give us the nourishment we need to sustain us on our journey. Mountains, in many traditional cultures, were considered to be sacred places, and even today some mountains are places of pilgrimage. Jesus often withdrew to the top of a mountain so that he could get away from the crowds and spend quality time with his father. We also need to take quality time out from the busyness of life to be recharged. That is the invitation in Psalm 23, where God our Good Shepherd shows his love and care for us by inviting us to bask in his presence.

> **He brought me out into a spacious place; he rescued me because he delighted in me.**
>
> Psalm 18:19

The Lord is my shepherd,
I shall not be in want.
He makes me lie down in green pastures,
he leads me beside quiet waters,
he restores my soul.

Psalm 23:1–2

In our culture, we use one minute of silence
as a way of respectfully remembering those
who have died. But silence itself is deeply
refreshing for body, mind and spirit, so it
is a habit we should learn to cultivate any
time, anywhere. It is also in the silence
that we really learn the art of listening and
can discover the next landmark for the
journey.

There is a space within all of us,
a quiet place reserved for God.
Here, we can listen to his voice,
receive his love
and bask in his presence.
Go to that place now.
Rest,
relax,
and enjoy.

With all my heart I praise the Lord!
I will never forget how kind he has been.
The Lord forgives our sins,
heals us when we are sick,
and protects us from death.
His kindness and love
are a crown on our heads.
Each day that we live,
he provides for our needs
and gives us the strength
of a young eagle.

Psalm 103:2–5

SILENCE IS...

A space in time to retreat.
A place to grow, to be watered and fed.
To learn only those things
that flourish
in its soil.

To embrace change, we need to leave the secure behind and
journey towards the future, knowing we can make a difference.

The fruit of silence is prayer.
The fruit of prayer is faith.
The fruit of faith is love.
The fruit of love is service.

Mother Teresa

PEACE PRAYER   May the peace of God encircle you,
May the peace of Christ enfold you,
May the peace of the Spirit encompass you
This day and for evermore.

Nothing in all creation is so like God as stillness.

Meister Eckhart

MOUNTAINS AND VALLEYS

Those who can scale the heights are those who have first learned how to survive in the depths.

Our journey through life is not one long party. There are many ups and downs along the way, as well as long periods of time when nothing seems to be happening.

Sometimes there are potholes, peat bogs and dead ends; but there are also lush valleys and ravines which provide oases of refreshment. Nobody ever promised us a problem free life. Even Jesus' ministry was beset with problems from beginning to end. But whatever we go through we know that we are not alone, because God promises to be our companion along the way: *'Though I walk through a valley of deepest darkness, I fear no harm, for you are with me'* [Psalm 23:4]. It is in the valleys of difficulty and hardship that our faith really grows, and if we surrender our problems to God, he can transform our *'Valley of Trouble into a gateway of hope'* [Hosea 2:15].

To experience suffering is to embrace the vulnerability of mankind and to touch the heart of God.

Whenever trouble comes your way, let it be an opportunity for joy. For when your faith is tested, your endurance has a chance to grow.

James 1:2–3

Every painful event contains in itself a seed
of growth and liberation.

Anthony de Mello

hope springs

Hope
springs
through
the hard
ground
of winter
cracking the earth
with her silent beauty.
An explosion of decadent colours
and outrageous plumes of foliage.
From bulb to shoot and shoot to bloom
her beauty cannot be arrested.
Even the hard frost of winter
cannot alter her course,
for hope will always
break through.

Let not your heart be troubled, neither let it be afraid.

John 14:27

Suffering helps us to discover who or what we are truly trusting in, and to uncover our real purpose and destination in life.

Every valley shall be raised up,
every mountain and hill made low;
the rough ground shall become level,
the rugged places a plain.
And the glory of the Lord will be revealed,
and all mankind together will see it.

Isaiah 40:4–5

God whispers in our pleasures, speaks in
our conscience, but shouts in our pains; it
is his megaphone to rouse a deaf world.

C S Lewis

H

I   T

n   G

My   N

Weakness   E

Lies   R

My   T

Greatest   S

My grace is sufficient for
you, for my power is made
perfect in weakness.

2 Corinthians 12:9

CREATIVE LANDSCAPES

The beauty of creation has inspired many of our finest artists to create their greatest works of art.

In the Bible we are described as *'God's masterpiece'* – his greatest achievement (Ephesians 2:10). We, like our Master Creator, all possess creative gifts which must find their natural expression if we are to fulfil our creative potential. For many people creativity emerges during the darker, more barren periods of their lives. My career as a writer began when I was ill with ME (Chronic Fatigue Syndrome). I never dreamt that God would transform that valley of darkness into a doorway of hope, both for me and for others who have since benefited from my writings.

THE AUTHOR

Today is a blank page for me to fill,
but the faintest line
or the smallest dot
is not my authorship,
for I am held in the palm of the Master
whose signature is written
across all creation.

Life informs art. But faith inspires works of art.

I want to be useful or bring enjoyment to all people. And therefore I am so grateful to God for giving me this gift of writing, of expressing all that is in me!

Anne Frank

SOUNDSCAPE

What is sound
but visual poetry
painted across the landscape of heart and mind
etched in time
to creation's rhythm.

Many things can be taught, but real art comes from the soul.

SOUNDWAVES

My soul cries through music
in notes I don't have words for
and the melody is carried
on the airwaves of sound.

Hope is hearing the melody of the future. Faith is to dance it.

Rubem Alves

DANCING

What is dance
but an explosion of raw energy
charged with emotion
electric in passion
trained to precision.

More lyrical than any poem,
more expansive than any landscape,
the dancer paints
in lines and colours,
shades and textures
of unimaginable beauty.

A divine union
of body, soul and spirit.
Creator and created
dancing
as
one.

WATERSCAPE

Stars of light
sprinkled like
p e p p e r
magnify
the mystery
of hidden depths.

But ocean's secrets

remain.

MOONLIT PATHWAYS

The moon writes its signature
in charcoal fingers across the
sky.
Ribbons of light unveil

a

stepping

stone

tapestry

in

mirrored waters.

Dance is a metaphor
for the human spirit
in absolute freedom.

WALKING ANCIENT PATHWAYS

We have much to learn from those who have gone before us – our

spiritual ancestors. The Celts believed that every spring, river, lake,

mountain and forest was a sanctuary

representing sacred space.

> Your people
> will rebuild
> the ancient
> ruins, and
> will raise up
> the age-old
> foundations.
>
> Isaiah 58:12

Celtic spirituality
maintains this respect
for creation together
with the sense of God's
presence in everything.
The simple lifestyle of the Celts
together with the strength of their
faith in God inspires us to keep
going however tough the journey.

St Cuthbert, a seventh-century
monk and former bishop of
Lindisfarne wrote:

'If I could live in a tiny dwelling on
a rock in the ocean, surrounded by
the waves of the sea and cut off

from the sight and sound of everything else, I would still not be free of the cares of this passing world, or from the fear that somehow the love of money might still come and snatch me away.'

St Patrick's Breastplate is a wonderful prayer for protection on life's journey:

Christ be with me
    Christ within me
Christ behind me
    Christ before me
Christ beside me
    Christ to win me
Christ to comfort
    and restore me
Christ beneath me
    Christ above me
Christ in quiet
    Christ in danger
Christ in hearts of
    all that love me
Christ in mouth of
    friend and stranger.

There is little point in focusing on the past
unless we use it to redefine our future.

LIFELINES

Our lives move
in straight lines
along the pages
of time.
The ink leaves its mark… across
the generations.

An open book for all to read.

CURBER EDGE

These granite rocks
are my cathedral,
my monastery.
Their sheer faces
jut out into the valley below,
directing my path.

A refuge for the traveller,
a haven for birds.

Time weathered stones
to rest
and to nest
with so many ancient stories to tell.

We call upon
the Sacred Three
to save, shield and surround
this house, this home,
this day, this night
and every night.

From the Brigid Blessing

Wisdom is supreme; therefore get wisdom.
Though it cost all you have, get understanding.
Esteem her, and she will exalt you;
embrace her, and she will honour you.

Proverbs 4:7–8

Lord, kindle in my heart
a flame of love to my neighbour,
to my enemies, my friends,
my kindred all,
from the lowliest thing that liveth
to the name that is highest of all.

From the Brigid Blessing

I weave into my life this day
the presence of God upon my way.

Source unknown

BOUNDARIES AND BRIDGES

When certainties disappear, a whole range of new possibilities appear.

On our journey through life there are likely to be many boundaries and bridges. Boundaries are important, because without boundaries we are liable to wander off course.

Without boundaries in our relationships there is likely to be little respect. Sometimes on our journey we may encounter obstacles that bring us to a standstill. Unforgiveness can be one of these obstacles. The people who hurt us most are often those closest to us, but if we refuse to forgive them it can be a real stumbling block and may affect future friendships as well as our relationship with God. Bitterness can become a permanent roadblock which prevents us from travelling any further. But we need to 'Love until it hurts' as Mother Teresa reminds us. The Bible tells us to *'continue to love one another, for love comes from God '* (1 John 4:7). Forgiveness is a decision: we can choose to forgive or not. But if we do, we offer both ourselves and our adversaries a bridge that can set both parties free. For we are warned that if we do not forgive others, we will not be forgiven! *'But if you do not forgive men their sins, your Father will not forgive your sins'* (Matthew 6:14–15).

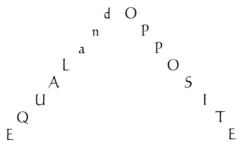

EQUAL and OPPOSITE

forces rule our lives.
We are drawn towards the truth
but tempted by evil.
We buckle under pressure
and snap when tension mounts.
But if God is our bridge,
stability is assured
because he is our load-bearer
allowing us to walk free.

PERSONAL
BRIDGES

We are the bridges between the old and the new
between one generation and the next,
drawn forever onward
into a future embracing
love and hope.
An eternal destiny heavenward.

Forgiveness is not an occasional act,
it is a permanent attitude.

Martin Luther King

Love is patient, love is kind.
It does not envy,
it does not boast,
it is not proud.
It is not rude,
it is not self-seeking,
it is not easily angered,
it keeps no record of wrongs.
Love does not delight in evil
but rejoices with the truth.
It always protects,
always trusts,
always hopes,
always perseveres.

1 Corinthians 13:4–7

Fear closes a door but faith pushes it
right open.

When my mind, body and spirit
are reconnected with God,
I know that I've
Come home.

I will say of the Lord,
'He is my refuge and my fortress,
my God, in whom I trust.'

Psalm 91:2

May the strength of God pilot us,
May the power of God preserve us,
May the wisdom of God instruct us,
May the hand of God protect us,
May the way of God direct us,
May the shield of God defend us,
May the host of God guard us against
   the snares of evil
and the temptations of the world.

St Patrick

God's text is
a message that
says I luv U
unconditionally.

TOUCHING GRACE The greatest

demonstration of grace – God's love in action – was when God

sent his son Jesus to die for our sins so that we might live.

In so doing, God allowed his son to become
the bridge between earth and heaven. The cross
is the place where pain and suffering meet hope
and transformation, the bridge between this life
and the next – where the impossible becomes
possible and death gives birth to new life.

TOUCHING
GRACE

Grace is all of love:

I experience her through others,
in creation
and within myself.

I experience her depths,
touch her energy,
live in her presence.

Her love shines through
laughter and tears,
forgiveness and reconciliation,
for she is all of love.

For it is by grace you have been saved, through faith…
it is the gift of God.

Ephesians 2:8

Whosoever loves much can accomplish much,
and what is done with love is well done.

Vincent van Gogh

Set me as a seal on your heart
as a seal upon your arm;
for love is as strong as death,
passion relentless as the grave.
Its flashes are flashes of fire,
the very flame of the Lord.

Song of Songs 8:6–7

Kind words can be short and easy to speak,
but their echoes are truly endless.

Mother Teresa

YOUR LOVE

Your love hovers and broods
over the waters
The sweetest of sounds echoing
across oceans

m i l e s

LOVE OF GOD

Love of God
Enfold me.

Spirit of God
Renew me.

Power of God
Infuse me.

Love alone lightens every burden, and makes the rough places smooth. It bears every hardship as though it were nothing, and renders all bitterness sweet and acceptable.

Thomas à Kempis

Feed the hungry and
help those in trouble.
Then your light will shine out from the darkness,
and the darkness around you shall be as bright as day.
The Lord will guide you continually,
watering your life when you are dry
and keeping you healthy too.
You will be like a well-watered garden,
like an ever-flowing spring.

Isaiah 58:10–11

Do all the good you can,
By all the means you can,
In all the ways you can,
In all the places you can,
To all the peoples you can,
As long as ever you can.

John Wesley

ETERNAL ECHOES

We move through our lives like pilgrims on a journey, heading for our destination. But as that journey nears its end, we realize that death is not a terminus, but a junction.

It is a gateway between the fulfilment of our lives here on earth and a new beginning. Beyond this border country, a whole new landscape opens up and we discover that this is where our real adventure begins.

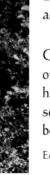

God has made everything beautiful for its own time. He has planted eternity in the human heart, but even so, people cannot see the whole scope of God's work from beginning to end.

Ecclesiastes 3:11

Those who know where they are going in eternity are able to make the most impact here on earth.

Stephen Gaukroger

As weeds push their way through concrete, so life will always burst through the hard ground of death.

AN OPEN DOOR

The door of childhood remains open for ever
for those who have eyes to see
beyond man-made limitations
to adventure on the open sea.

Don't store up for yourselves treasures on earth, where moth and
rust destroy...but store up for yourselves treasure in heaven...
for where your treasure is, there your heart will be also.

Matthew 6:19–21

High
on a mountain's
highest ridge I saw an
uncharted landscape open up
before me. Ice blue peaks perforating
the skyline of my experience. Like pillars of
wisdom towering above me, they point the way heavenward.

ETERNAL JOURNEYS

The landscape of our lives
bears the wounds of the One
who created us.
Seared through with love
we are beckoned homeward.

God is an infinite circle whose centre is everywhere
and whose circumference is nowhere.

St Augustine

May the road rise to meet you;
may the wind be always at your back.
May the sun shine warm upon your face,
and the rain fall soft upon your fields.
Until we meet again,
may God hold you
in the hollow of His hand.

Northumbria Community

Whoever finds me finds life.

Proverbs 8:35

JOURNEY'S END

THE END...
Or is it the beginning of a new journey
that stretches out before me,
an uncharted sea
that no one has returned from
except the One
who leads.

Jesus said 'I am the resurrection and the life. Those who believe in me, even though they die like everyone else, will live again. They are given eternal life for believing in me and will never perish.'

John 11:25–6

You can contact
the author on
liz@lizbabbs.com
or via her website
www.lizbabbs.com

TRACK TITLES

THE JOURNEY

TRAVELLING LIGHT

SACRED SPACE

MOUNTAINS AND VALLEYS

CREATIVE LANDSCAPES

WALKING ANCIENT PATHWAYS

BOUNDARIES AND BRIDGES

TOUCHING GRACE

ETERNAL ECHOES